The Tree Kept Growing

Joy Zummell

Edited by Candace Freeman

Library of Congress Control Number: <u>2015948247</u>
[Windsail Publishing], [Lincoln, DE]

ISBN-10:1943071004
ISBN-13:978-1-943071-00-5

DEDICATION

This book is dedicated to Clarence and Dorothy Cartwright, loving parents and grandparents.

ACKNOWLEDGMENTS

This is the true story of how love for a tree endured decades and beyond.

When Grandma was a little girl and Grandpa was a little boy, Grandpa planted a tree in his family's front yard.

Sometimes children played too close to it.

And someone walked
too close to it.

So Grandpa helped the tree and

placed a tire around it.

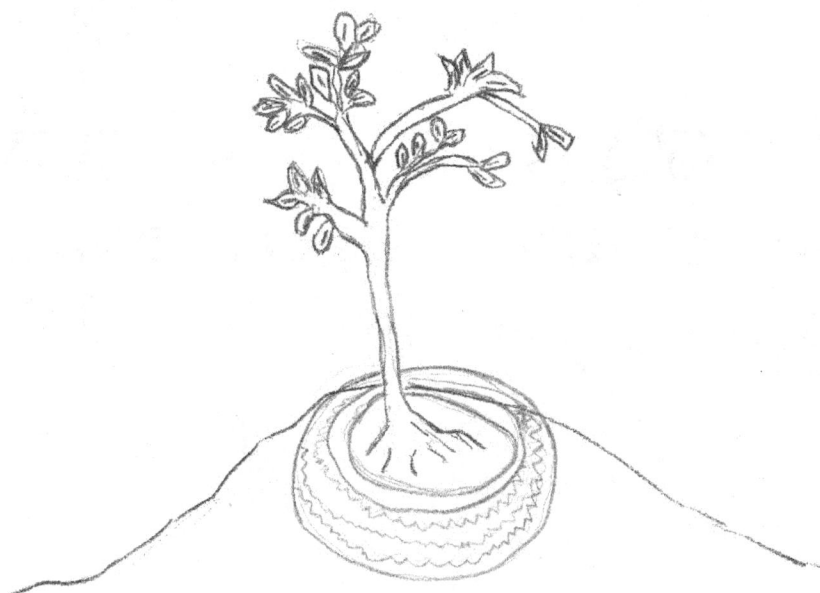

4

Every year the tree grew taller and larger. It was growing when Grandpa got his first job.

S

After Grandma married
grandpa, their first baby
was born.
The tree kept growing.

When Grandma and Grandpa started their first church, the tree was growing.

When Grandpa passed away, the tree was still growing.

Children and grandchildren can see the tree. Friends can see the tree. It is still growing…

...and growing.
Grandma enjoys the
tree that Grandpa
planted!

This is *not* the End!